BOOK OF VISIONS

POLYRHYTHMIC POEMS OF LOSS ABOUT SEX, DRUGS, AND ALIENS

Oliver Kelly

goin' to buy me a 6 shooter

the old man liked to suffer.
he was much younger than he suspected.
an unawareness can grip,
which seems like a force exterior.
he chews freshly used coarsely ground coffee beans
after dinner when all the coffee is gone.
he does not eat white bread.
only exercises his arms, neck, and stomach.
has perfect legs.
he expects a better waistline every season every year
but will not buy a new belt.
he glues his shoes,
picks at the glue.
solely – 4 black shirts and 2 black pants,
yellow socks.
has beer and hardboiled egg in his cheeks.
he's the rhinestone cowboy,
notches to fill with
more notches.

denim witch

all night dental youth program

desperado angrily tuning witch massacre into every radio,

time traveling blast.

"zer should be a rahide up eer ain it?"

grab the nuts,

compact the depressed dolphin.

hot night in every south wet town,

shorts up to fish

feet stinking in high heels in bubblegum,

red clay toes and tanning oil.

Tennessee 1987,

the gory crust.

lost god

a carpeted abstraction for temporal doom
man puking in a drain hole
though he's dug the trench unto it

people wanted to know
who's in that band
so now the band is just one person
and no one knows who plays the music

emaciated gatherings
folding liquid attempts at madness
curling fluid in attentive fluctuation of negative
infinite
rumble past the gods
they never toiled their soil for food
how are they better
without a home just
lonesome chariots

polluted

as the ashes of the discarded Canaanite newborns
adorn the industrial sewer walls of ancient past
so paint our ruined houses with the
maverick of white pebble.
for, when happened upon, the eye is slow to
accommodate the vision of such,
to pick from the disaster
the reason for horror.

how would you not cling to cotton
and the scent it must soak in
when washed pure?
it is the great advancement of
sewage and bones
to sweat in our clothed caves
moving   twisting   motioning
the sex of necessity,

whored beetles
and the need to get stoned
and buried in the instance of death.
into this our eyes
are forming,

a tainted charge
of whiskey and animal bones
at the verge of origin
in convulsive steam.

bye, John. so long, Capernaum.

these are solemn woes

which grieve the burier

hasten the fun

'til dawn returns

unacknowledged

and irretrievable

though we assume

it's weight

is eternal

and its master

off to another love

and its height

undying

with no need for mist

or of gain

running guiltless

in your guilty

until you beg for rain.

the danger of siding with an opposite as total reality

we from space
have learned to use the stars to create a vehicle
to transport illuminators' awareness
as your body,
a car made of fuel.
creel trail tucking two does
in the once green rumble,
a safe place in all directions,
and water
dark green
itself the reason for the Forest Green crayon
flowing through
soft over the rocks
not running them smooth with vigor
rather lying with them in the heat of winter
upon the water,
a car made of fuel.

people walk into a store
and are absorbed by other worlds.
this is a linear connection
electric consciousness
travelling,
a car made of
fuel.

a wolf in Paris prepares verses

loveless hunger for infantile radiation
crotches in limbo rest indentured
word virus the thoughts coming as
skeptical as first undressing
never enough first times
blood on the keys

we're running out of letters
squeeze squeeze legs together

chastise the cactus
you owe it all to nemesis
cumming pelvic bones that hit the ground and
sprout cacti in the humid afterlife
of dust and aggregation
it is not settled as the desert
little buds in the sand
bombs in the wind
ever gliding to the last man
the answers

the blood on the keys
squeeze squeeze legs together
balls in your seat blood on the keys
balcony arrangements of thrusting authority
blinding heat white and magic

greatest contest winner stepping forward
out drop his eyes replaced by medal
it's a...I think it's...it is! the reward is blue!

if I could botox one thing it would be this joint

none eye flicked and nimble
Latin dimensions bright and sturdy
fur tang in acrobatics plus.
the inverse inferior
reflection is an invention
attributed to consciousness
but memory is instinct
humming a flaw of flock model.

apply variance grudgingly
smell of turkey
escape science fiction drawing
in carpeted rooms
exploding hatches appear
while talks
about things
sedative.
elfin disagreeable arms
ranting gums into teeth and

the smell of toes all around
with no water
no ashes
the opaque motion of absence
without humor dancing,
running still as water appears.

I'm glad we haven't met

yesterday I woke up early,
exercised upside-down strenuously,
practiced tai chi,
changed the broken handles
on the driver's side of my van,
the door handle (first to go)
and the manual window,
replaced the bald wires with two new tires and a used one,
went to the grocery store and bought eggs,
boiled all of them,
peeled them,
did laundry,
wrote a few long poems
and took several notes for others,
wrote two songs,
picked up the flea medicine,
gave it to the dog,
bought her food,

fed,
worked,
made money,
rolled one,
and ate the world
with no one in it.

phonetic reversal CHIME

Morning tang of
smelling salts
scratched from anus,
all night communication,
symphonic tongues,
unwritten language dispelled
under weight of humanoid
eager for prosperity and the way.
Blue letters, relics,
not so ancient to
millennium-an-hour culture.
But she loses sleep.

Eyelashes cut with no root attached,
take only what you have
to need to kill.

                              purple lines
                              over mustard,
                              faded turquoise
                              cut from sand
                              and snake eyes,
                              risen peoples,
                              we speak.*

**Chime smell.

The furnace walls can take more.

Elevator waits.

          * capes you sell,

           pope and sire,

           see your cans.

           DNA, DNAs morph,

           tuck,

           saw,

           you cut

           dead off.

           drat! some river!

           senile,

           help her up.

Shukosikameinus-ensinkaubone-inthis-caus-au-krominatrix-ish-om-tak.

Stare.

Rot a veil.

"Ah, he Rome,"

cat knacks law.

He can ruff it.

Limbs emit.**

           Skin off, nod a coo.

starving in silk, surrounded by alien squirrel alarms

knew not of pineapple when it reached our shore

yellow as the tulip's Sun

sweetest

life from another planet

traveled in a vessel of space

Venus in spores

elements

catastrophes benevolent

life represented

from elsewhere

beyond the flame

direction

like shackles

masturbating with rough wounds
and soppy band-aids
confused ointment
cuts on fingers where smooth used to be
when

shill mashed banana
new veins in forehead
a day with many memories

fastened
void of history
snow figurines
hunting mother
searching her craft
for something under the twigs

hands under butt cheeks
and buckled thighs
fastened
void of history

and plastic holly berries
what are we doing there
in a stranger's back yard -

nothing but turning around

clear or never there

this moon burns knowingly
light blending the beast
shadow and fence
trees blinking unshaken Mars
clouds allegiant to die
lit green fag pinched with fingers slowly soaring
in an arch down the sky
a rabbit fondling in the bushes
beast aware
pale blue, the faded dark
the wrapped comet falling through and out of eye

education system, mountain of cracked eggs

there are stories of those malnourished
of Zen and in hastening search
wherein they eventually awaken in
a moment of realizing the simple
or abstract or material answer of a guru
but for a Buddha this is constantly happening
though seldom in even increments of oscillation

cocaine spiders and crow-shaped tigers
in a den of humbled and forgotten men
all crawling from a creaking head
heart strapped to it from the floor
ventricles and tentacles stapled to each

twang twang goes the heartstring
creak creak goes the head
ventricles and tentacles
in a den of humbled and forgotten men

"should" aisle island

neural flush in waves
electro and magnetic pulses
replacing, imitating
and conjuring
material for consumption
the primal instinct
to survive has pushed them further
away
(we're talking LIGHT here, shitheads)
and now we're the
material for consumption
stuffed teddy bears
on a rotating shelf

land where
you never have to hold onto anything
lesson of foreign hands in infancy
guided by a world filled with stores

the only way to get a couple
of generations of free-thinkers
to activate in a war storm
is let them fill each others' heads
with every idea, conspiracy,
possible reality, and death available,

some with a little truth in there,
a touch of nature and wisdom,
so they'll all come running when
hungry,
to fight for their own reality,
a computer killing itself.

the sun is round
in your eyes and
not without.

unpenetrable, killing business and the synergetic shadow

it's 2015
and the only president that could bring the troops home
from war business
left office before his son.

we're in the 6th stage of mass extinction
heavy on distinction when it comes to species who
survives.
but it's funny to think it stops there,
little dying frogs in dinosaur shit.

there's a square spaceship in my yard
though not always seen
until I remember in moments
how to fit inside
the lines of color the bubbles flow within
what it's like to fly through as cargo,
almost Midwestern.

how the two expressed
what we know as love
between white sheets

curly locks blue eyes to brown
they say to one another
"I don't know," and
"I don't know" you back.
and everything hears
that their heart is in it

miles between now just miles.

need a companion so you care?

scruffy grey puppy in the autumn sun,
sweater weather, sitting in the grass
getting hit in the head with a big leaf
every once in a while,
gazing out and smelling without
bothersome summertime panting

everything in life is leading to erectile dysfunction
the people you meet and don't meet
walking by, talking too loudly, scars and smells of
chronic masturbation with speckled hands and
jittery twitches of anxious complexion
all around.
the trough is buried
and the food is a mystery.

earth delivery from mars, something for the ice to chew on

you can't unload the sands here.
　　　　"well, it's our only stop
　　　　and what we got is sand."
where the hell are we going to put it?
we have no land.
　　　　"well, build it with sand."
land of sand?
how will anything walk upon it?
　　　　"they will have to wait until it hardens.
　　　　in the mean time, they will grow in size with
　　　　the strength of the sand."

well, can you throw in a little
cactus? fungus? anything flora for us?
　　　　"sure, alright, we'll send it zooming in.
　　　　nothing will know what hit 'em.
　　　　but, if they get too big
　　　　so will our packaging

　　　　and it could be detrimental,
　　　　catastrophic really."
shit, we've grown big in the sea.
if you send it too hard
you'll blow yourselves up,
34 million miles and everything between.
　　　　"well you can't grow too big

for impact in regards to how far

we are from you."

well, space is an issue,

haha.

"I guess you got me there. hahaha

alright, bring it in, people. dump it anywhere.

it'll drift around and settle like shit anyhow.

probably won't see you again

unless I live long enough

to get into politics."

won't all fit, sir.

"well, make a pile that orbits

and we'll fill it in where it settles later.

by the way

that's what happens when you go to someone else –

you come back.

you are always a continuous flow of, energy we'll call it,

from yourself to a body."

ah, don't start in with your Martian religion.

"religion? it's the past.

alright boys, come on.

I'm done with this

fish."

fish?   what color are you?

"fish."

you're no fish.

       "well neither are you. it isn't possible

       to be personal. but, really

       fuck this place. you'll all be dead and morphed into

       little whatever-we-come-up-withs when I'm barely reaching

       middle age

       so just be glad you're not one of them down there trying to

       learn to

       like worms."

well, you could have given them

something more appetizing.

       "space is an issue, my dear."

space is an issue.

aternal meatus

if you're a dick around friends and they applaud
you're either worth it or they're bad friends.

I was raised in a lens
problem point not
to more lenses added to my sole given
but life should not be viewed through lenses
because it is not a camera.

it is sole given,
problem point not,
mechanism for capturing images
frames roll
in agreeable flow
of height.
there is no ceiling where there is no floor.
you could eat off that rhythm.

at the end I'll still be sure you will write my story
but you, hallway through, wouldn't let me write a copy

mining for magic
though the cave be protected by aluminum and guns
and the magic a switch

families-proud-of-being-families culture

born and fucked into privilege

of faux accomplishment standard,

disgusting people with the same itchy ass

buying organic places

unveiled as a graveyard

they never know.

die on the way next time.

when you've been in one town too long

you become an experiment,

black helicopters flying over in the night

real fast

and outside they send in tobacco

then beer

and it becomes a tobacco town or a beer town

but tobacco is another experiment

and the beer is just regular water to those

out

there.

I am always at this desk

no matter the movement,

changes in scenery,

level of blipping light, smoke, or power.

at this desk is always where I am.

it is my store, my grave, disruptive vacation key,

alimony in a stamp redesigned for an envelope

not yet invented,

simultaneously my sin and predecessor,

red and aconite.

it is raising me from childhood

solidifying my monument

entombing my beggar

in a journey of travels worldwide

universal

complete

though presence be a desk

this is my always.

I could can Cheetos and reinvent grain,

hear China and trace cave mushrooms.

should I leave I shall remain.

typing out lives in three second increments,

pressing into a loop that

repeats the last three minutes of everyone's lives

flickering a faux existence in their last steps and breaths,

pretending childhood,

trauma, and dinner,

so that each one regains their pain

over and …over and …over .

I will stick you into a motion of continuously crashing,

smashing your finger, and hungering of poverty and loneliness.

into enough contrast characters die –

fin d'existence, mrityor with question of

fluid.

has traction/chapped soled bitch in a peach carbon sweater

indecent cartoons do not exist,
for if their clothes were removed
or any of their actions blurred into paper
they would disappear.

cheap cans of tuna and eggs
with kim chee and soy sauce,
spices and greens and beans.
cheap cans of tuna and eggs
in a salad.
cheap cans of tuna and eggs
in a baked frittata.
cheap cans of tuna and eggs
with salt and black pepper,
maybe some mushrooms
and bell peppers.
cheap cans of tuna and eggs
with dill.
a cartoon is a cartoon.

stinking of your child's palms,
grassed Armageddon,
"Om" sound from the sea of pickles
stuck in a sea of rube mouths,

deepthroat water the lawn

with rabies

and biocatalytic enthymeme.

your strong opinion is my heart

I remember we'd drive half an hour, maybe more
to the only coffee shop around
just to get nearer to the magic we felt
had to be available
somehow
in a corner with wooden walls.
it was disgusting and cost all our money in gas,
but we were desperate to find
something.
I feel the end closing
but then
it was fresh.

We die there
sometimes.

what can I do with a viola besides masturbate in tune?

shitting in the bar
shitting in the bank
have class to your danger
and a feeling for mystery
like the desert knows the sea
as beyond the mountains
and the sea understands the deserts
still, familiar air.
hold a mutual fear
of the barriers falling
into a tropical sex
of ancient recalculation,
friction of fiery submission.
flush.
keep the corners dry when you're done.
don't worry about humming me to sleep tonight;
a switch uses a lot of pieces.
a switch is made of a lot of pieces too.

roy rogers

they've mapped the spider's web,

the asteroid lines of orbit around our winged cage,

and we care about our hair and career goals –

the resistance –

the shoes and socks –

the sexual sex –

the non-sexual sex –

the aptitude of taste-tests –

the logical lack of consciousness

in the dwelling magnetic tide.

sitting on the concrete

under buzzing fluorescent parking lot lights

we eat childhood French fries

and find our fathers' faces inside

getting ketchup –

(the sauce in time we

found we could demand)

red in steam and love,

amongst the crowd outside

amongst the crowd outside outside.

due to the hole in the top of native American teepees

the sun was forcefully intense in tents. (in tents?

intense?) how did Natives avoid sunburns?

in tense.

sick of you standing naked in the kitchen

a dream in a pocket of white
I run grenades through your hair
knuckling wrinkles hot and tight
with the bloating fear of sexual plastic
in an unhurried jungle.
I am never awake in the kitchen
but we all stand there naked among the god
dreaming in grenade
of our Earth.

though realism the most painstaking to capture

it is barely art.
worked hard this life to pedestal
outcries of infamy
so that no one will every time again pay attention
this have we toiled with the abundance of seeming life
limited ourselves
with all the non-art consumed
radiated back as bad art

and you can't drown out the blues
with a dishwasher.

paint your shirt
and clothe your eyes when you dry,
reflect, read, write, or shit.
grunt-fuck a masterpiece
but don't let anyone see it,
though you're proud of
what the body has formed
on the porcelain canvas.

being hunted makes you common

Li Po had it right,

get rid of all the good information

because the putrid humans are coming to learn

and if you can get rid of the most beneficial things

it's a true "fuck you" to all of humankind.

if it seems a suicide

I've been killed by a ghost.

we're at war,

and I'm the ghost-killer.

the unfairness of the living

fuels my hate into beautiful things

and the ghosts understand that.

but, they want my house,

the same I've freely shared,

and they're moving my fingers now.

all you writers, philosophers,

artists: beware.

thrust through

bare feet in raw eggs, the jelly oozing over fleshy toes,
things that should not go together in a bowl
but the sunlight puts them there together like fruit.

cousin huffing cottage cheese
opens the door to a bigger outside
a larger her
in the pants of the young
purple and onions
staining prepubescent vaginas
in tainted hunger
for the lost fluff
gurgling hums of gums and cancer,
read them,
they
the young;
for they will tender
the rude awakening
because time,
though still,
moves

as a building with a bottom story filled with water
in a prison housing sweet men
now destined to violence and clam,
the worst eyes awaiting there,

so scary because they used to be good eyes
 a truck going by once a day to spray down
the entire building.

the level made of water shrinks,
and the whole building falls a story quickly
and then slowly rises back up,
terror in the name of cleanliness.
there is nothing purple about this yellow
though there is knowledge of veins.

holy ghost legs

I made it into yoghurt without anyone looking.
she was bent over washing her hair with her long toes in the river
and I was watching her legs,
the muscles move like they naturally should;
it was unnoticed electric current.
and no one saw the wrinkles form in her soles as she contemplated
each movement.
it was an ark built before the commanding eyes
of a god almighty
and no one could take away
the thought of completion
in the cunt of regeneration
and the anointing of the time we've spent together in oil.
she has cum up there
and she is saving it.
it is not mine.
and some get the feeling at that moment
of pure arousal she contains **halcyon death** –

fully shared consciousness in a dome of epipsychidion,
never-ending patterns to melt together blanketing over,
there is no mirage but a common elysian holographic hope
the blanket will not be there after the next perception.

but, they just feel something.

and that sad arousal
that sad arousal
that sad arousal.

sweet tooth

the walk through video stores of your past

in sequential often

little rooms of harmonic throat singing overlay

tape on walls and empty cases

echo new beginnings to eventual boredom

carpet clean on the bottom of shoes synthetic squawk

has a feeling of chewing dry paper towels

afraid to watch the movie on the multiple televisions too long

taking shirt off in the employee bathroom to play with your own

boobs

become the movies the tape

deliquesce the hard sugar

genesis of a candy kid.

"If I am here now

it is only because I was still here when

I realized to what extent the world

had worsened." – Paul Bowles – An American In Tangier

astronomical amount of bananas

clouding an unearthly horizon

blinking yellow

haunting amounts of potassium

oozing inside

creating a wall

over your new sun

bend over and stay there put bananas in your hair

willing

fall is the time for please smoke cigarettes

your perception
by nature
is unusual

a fear of
an artist -

he jumped up from the chair
ending a haircut and exclaimed a fear
a danger a threat from the surrounding
bombardment of reality in question
and consciousness speculative
"Imagine if you were static –
you'd always look the
same!"
his white hair on the floor
dark oncoming winter
closing the day early outside.

as I drive home
the women are all static
I can smell them in their houses
doing things I've loved about a few
that turned to torment

44

castrating as iron

the visibility between

and I hurry home to eat breakfast

on a night in oblivion

mezzo limbo

a vat of colchicine and vitriol

in a hotel of buzzing

purchased flowers

we still sorry

children with green faces

kneeling at the fireplace

of a doomed

brick house

Jimmy Dean

Yell at the kid,

"Hey you fuckers,
get your dicks out of the
refrigerator and into
the god damn microstoven."
Everyone baffled,
they each pick a blunt object
and race for one another with
all their chemicals stun-set.
Good morning, juice.
Lay on the floor, you
were happier in the dirt anyhow.

It's started,
a whole day like this
and I want to crawl into the nook
and take my breath away,
come back as a pig,
just like them. Then,
they'd all eat my sausage after the fight.
They would rip into it, sinking jaws
into every scrap piece of body.
Everything would be flesh scented from the pan.

No wall would refuse the odor,

no saliva withdraw from the temptation to run.
Keep it in the kitchen,
it belongs there.

I am a click attending/
clinical defeat looking for needle

I want to dream in slick-page magazine

pale figures in strong lighting

colors pure in the rays

images for nothing

calling to you

replacing the word

eating your immunity.

the delinquent radiation

of a younger universe

bedridden with adolescence

with a pre-vocabulary

of infinite thought,

a diagram for new disaster

to form together

an obliteration,

a breathing of cosmic abundance

and reflection

with nothing living too long

or ever dying,

acne.

blue river over autumn pebbles

I have brought holiday peace with a bow of loneliness

it is an avid relief not to participate

there is no fun only illusory digression into haunted wont

by the charm of Armageddon I bow and unwrap candied tears

ambulances turning off sirens around the bushes

eating sugar as a country to stay alive

palms and hands of wasps in atoms oiled

pills for the elderly to hand out candy and buy cheap trinkets

appreciated like abuse and rubber tires

precious reclusive wrinkles choosing a special cheap necklace

for an ungrateful grandchild

giving up the good grocery for a little while

padded black shoes of elderly misery

a bruised recollection of shame and alchemy

humbled in wine and scotch with little mystery

and the light waits at the end

trickling fevers

binding redemption to unnecessary rocks

casting the idea away

a breathing liver saying "hello"

1st day in the dirt: the new ew

fingering out bacon,

death is a bubbled level.

old man lay there with his skin suit

buttoned into his spine,

hidden coffin secrets,

protruding bones and dry wires.

I said "Thank You,"

got behind the hearse.

it is evening,

and he looked like morning.

open her(e), carefully.

as a cat comes home

to bury clay, still calloused bodies

with suns in the backyard

never telling a soul,

you're safe, little animal.

acid on acid

a migration of mutants in an Epipsychidion of lotion
(of blood and palm)
trudging through realms of Mahandzhar and ubiquitous foams
round endeavor words the worm known

I walked too far and there were parrots
I knew but kept indexing my eyes
PARROTS! PARROTS!
they follow the lanky creatures always
the man and tiger with joints of conjuring forms eloquent as simple
silhouettes reducing matter to repetitious moans

I have been everywhere in this form
though it may periodically change
novels and reckless words regenerate scarcely paved madness
symbols in explosions come the parrots more
and then the worm follows
as it should as night
a Monday night covered in essence
of plight and miserable night
wet from all it's engorged
a follower weekend in vomit and workday rinsed clean
a worm on a dead parrot in the night
what else to eat on a Monday
I've been everywhere

smooth hand on the left and veins on the right

typing words on dead parrots

BANG! you're inked

BANG! dead parrot didn't know you had a tongue

BANG!

stamping parrots with a symbol

every key a new life banged dry

loading dock cafeteria

I'm still trying to enjoy the rebellion of adolescence
knowing a gunman is taking the building. seek the pretty tortured
girl and make sure the kitchen staff is appreciated and paid.
combat boots, denim, and flannel dreams are companion for peach
born popcorn chemtrails show your god when it is needed you see
it, black baby in Harlem dies for Detroit.

hofman juggling lsd in the sky with whatever savior you need
without it
up and cock holding the sea in true nightwatch
advantageous dismember
you need winter
no toilet paper stress
lsd shouldn't have planned first date
9 hours after last hit
knuckle bleeding don't remember doing that
don't remember crossing leg
old lady next to me whispers to her suave black-haired companion

"I am suddenly allergic to something in here"
need to flee
need the lsd to stop making sense
this can't be the date – my hair is not black
is it the dog fur on my coat she's blowing out her nose?

does she know her venture capitalism and soap fetish need malaria?

can she cope with strength in a corner of anxiety

I'm digging for her a tomb

in mental convulsions ex-wife needing drugs sending

hearts and valley I

need to climb can't confuse the lsd coffee

cannabis gabapentin bcaa ionic

magnesium shots of B duck eggs smoked salmon

mushrooms mental

convulsions in a corner of anxiety I'm digging for her a tomb

can she cope?

hanna waits before she answers

serous
beauty standing on
her porch
last word I heard from her was "soon"

pale with
Incognition
frost-blissed coat
warming
tempered doom

subastral elastic
buried our walker in
a mountain we feel
had just before been a hill
risen transcending
small places in fluid
anticipation coughed initial

her astringent nettles extract not
the darkness but its strength
shared love vanguard
keeping watch for a white room
rubbing the beauty over "soon" over "soon."

mingus moanin'

the only things that bring together the past and the present are
rhythm, love, and prison.

a child can read as scanning

the adults though few

but whose character remains

penetrable

of conditioning,

a section remaining unprogrammed you.

magnetic image (MRI)

may be taken of the rhythm of magnetic reactions

in a magnetic reality

mirroring itself with anti-matter,

self-aware as jazz,

blinker.

Plié

I say, "maybe we could put on a record."
The reply, "I just want your cock in my mouth."

Taking off her shoes,
brown tangled laces over worn, sandy leather,

she has dancer feet and flexes them with every sensation.
Sucking each red grape, the skin holding fast,
antioxidant,
she cums with a finger and particular vein.
True orgasms take time,
the best ingredient when something is already good.
Gripping the air between her toes
I see her calves twitch like a horse shewing
a fly that has been bothering it all day and
finally must leave. She washes away our sins and
I get a towel.

She immediately grabs a bottle of lotion she must have
found with a sort of radar and began working me over again.
She put me so far in her,
she vomited all over my cock and the bed sheets.
After a quick bath, running back into the room,
straddling the air between us,
she landed.
I penetrated something deeply foreign and she sang
Happy Birthday until I came again.

She was a dancer,
I was her stage.

Dennis the Menace

I (dick c. chix)

I was sitting in an American restaurant

eating shit-food by myself out of a trough

with some sort of confidence

I didn't understand.

From the facing trough,

I felt eyes.

She immediately hit on me

and offered some fun at her place.

Here?

She was attractive and putting herself

on a limb I couldn't help but swing from

for a little while.

She said "NO cheese,"

put her kid in a booster seat

and we got in her car

with the suggestion that I sit in the back.

Suddenly, a surreal blond

with semi-permeable skin emitting

the cheap taste of American country cuisine

got in through the passenger door,

plopped down and said "I've got cheese."

They were sisters,

one with stronger limits,

the other willing

to go to cheese level with me.
Who taught them this shit?
After quick discussion,
they agreed to both take me
and I hadn't said a word,
just staring and eventually
looking over at the kid
with empathetic bombardment
of familiar confusion,
both fastened in our places.
So, I was headed to Brevard,
a house of two sisters,
a kid,
and a guaranteed good time
overshadowed by delusion
and "cheese," "no cheese."
I was alright with my belt,
but aware.

"Are they all this way, Mommy?"
No one understood the little boy

sticking out his little devil tongue –
we were misled.
His focus was on the underside flow
of ejaculation.

At their house,

there was a party with a buffet,

family style –

I was in.

The Momma (no cheese) had

bright purple-red fake dyed hair

and shoved her tongue around

my cheeks while we loaded our plates –

the young blond waiting.

The kid grew.

II (screwge mcfuck)

Activate a crunch storm,

multi-task a fluid delivery –

it's all in the process,

blood massage.

I want to walk you home

in a separate building.

Cunt-handling a grab attack,

bathroom so filthy

you brush your teeth and get crabs.

Heat you feel varies your temperature.

  Her heat breathes.

Some teeth and hair make us all

a cartoon worth drawing.
Kick robotic
drink robotic
in a land of misfit toys.

I had a dream that
I couldn't wake up,

naked and cooking only
heavy vats of margarine
on a flattop grill,
seeing old girlfriends
and remembering why I liked them.
I fought with my body.

the age at which it is funny to think of your mother dying down stairs

when others create small talk
I only listen between words
and find love again
when it becomes silent.

there's a lesson in watching them
break their robot identity.
the best dogs are sterilized,
as will we soon follow like pets,
castrated and marked.

as with crime, drugs, and hindsight,
the way weight is lifted
determines its distribution.

the design of lubrication
dances
in tubes of
necessary appeal,
mimicking hunger
without feeling.

the extenuation of circumstances

not all regarding you

psychedelic

entrepreneur

devouring

the cure

goo you with rhythm-work to afford to forget it to return to work; you only need one pair of pants.

there was an explosion in the wormhole and our reality shifted,
dimensions left to new directions and we could still see a little,

though not with our eyes, hear a little, though not with ears:
smeared pupils of Arundhati as Serengheti spaghetti
in a childhood daydream,
three million years of taste
accumulating as vacuum dust
behind the eyelids of prehistoric weight.
the hopelessness of trying and not succeeding
and the fear that prevents trying at all
cringes the deeper parts,
and drugs break free the inhibition
to absolve limits that pound from the outside.
there is a system and then your own ideals.

you must choose your limits for participation in that system.

profit promise,
stability,
ownership,
success,
a standard.
a golden statue of ratty cum-dragons and cunty fuck-ribbons in
space,

dangling the anthropomorphic retrograde of the future in sound.

But you must bounce around
on the outside
and not take the path within,
the unlikely life in grooves of an American Quarter,
submerging with purpose not succumbing in fear and self-worth at
stake,

for the latter is participating in the circle system.

the system is flawed and if you fail in it you are not.

who can afford to live intentionally?
submerge yourself into participation

to see what you can get out of the system
and keep to the outside
and leave the premises if necessary.
the greatest fear I can approach
is having to realize that I am stuck here – that this is it – work,
shitty education,

get high and go back to work
where you aren't high enough
and your humanity is approached
in system standards
that disregard life,

get high and feel a little relief,

work,

headaches,

earth,

stale light

and smells of fluorescents in carpet fuzz

and filing cabinets in microchips

bleeding plastic

into (my) seas

from (the) apartment

where I sweat in the summer

if I'm lucky enough to live

to work, to get high enough to forget it, and return.

a book well written will be the guide to worship, fiction,

a day in the stars with breathable sight.

Live Music at Lonestar Bar

Don't lift your arms,

smell renegades.

The brown Ecuadorian boy just played

a song that colored his cheeks you.

I see response in your sweat.

Set your sails and ride

the wind.

Journey the sea with

a ten minute hot seat,

twist and grind,

I see you.

I see your ankles pressing

hard the earth,

not giving in so easily.

Whirl your frozen pieces,

stir the liquidation,

ice chunks meet stage eyes

under a toothpick

with hidden splinters.

Become food to devour.

He likes that,

true gourmand.

Release your condiments

with subtlety.

You're a strange color

for mayonnaise,

bending at the knees,

cream configuration –

the powers of the piano man.

Under the keys,

frugal dick-mutterings,

contempt for the insertable aneurysm,

vibrations Transfesa,

the dusty south transport.

His mind is back there

now, pretending you are her.

Fan-based orgasms,

deafening crowd of nothing alone.

She never stops sweating

and the boy sings stamina.

He was a lanky water-birth,

never forgetting sanctuary walls.

Return.

Only post-orgasm can one come

after they have already arrived.

When are they more present to engage,

to be appreciated

for insulated sensibility

under the brightness

of the most vulnerable interrogation?

Dropping a tip in the jar, sneaking,

she tasted him by the piano —

a dry-brushed green

harpsichord disappointment, sour.

She feared the deep cut drive-by,

must digress to outer states,

elsewhere,

and we are,

rejection.

He pulled her back in,

took her quick

behind the building,

misty, musky, and panting for a beer.

Shorts cut bootlegs for stuffing fist-first.

What is so fancy about sex

when it is all about the fuck?

Sledge the surface

ignoring the eggs within her.

Caress, dumper-dive the areas

they all neglect.

For, it will be

green bean casserole for every meal

thirty years later.

What did you eat from her back then?

One day,

wire through a cage

the package you always wished to send her.

One glance can leave eyes with memory.

Body temperature follows the retina.

Pudge-grabber's ink swells, a warning.

Walnuts for fat chicks,

give baking soda its meaning;

arise and get dirty.

She always pleases,

remembering his song.

Take a stamp, send a future.

We are dying in here,

staining all the clothes red.

Fade to black,

earthen.

White gin dribble-monkeys,

lonely as a heart attack –

Bury her beneath the strings

and keep playing to those

decomposed eyes.

Develop the free wind,
green-velvet-stuffy:
It's serious.

Tinkersmell cunt-shit a brownie
and can fly,
a funeral.

White Knuckle It

I am starting to have

superpower abilities

like having

an acute sense of what time it is

when I wake up

and where I drunkenly

last set my glasses

the night before.

Past the Down Syndrome tacos,

chief keef cheese quiche,

lemonade isle,

eating everything,

two sets of eyes

with a box of Tide

looking through –

on it a child

smiling at nothing left.

They sit there still

the morning after –

no stocking took place yet.

So I walk out of

the grocery store

I stole from last night,

cleaned my glasses

on the way out

with Windex
I left on the shelf,
and felt free –
the wind only
       always
         fills outside.
Don't suffocate.

getting high

I mean really high

down to the local market

there is a ghost in your house

and it may not follow you

eat a fish quick sand witch

back to the house

who fed you mushrooms

was it the fish

your friend made it

he works there

was it a hookup

a prank

a blessing

it feels like it all

not just any one thing

any one answer

and boxes are flying around the house

smashing into books

and the puppy is calm

but she is playing in my head too

fluttering fur in a sunlight not appropriate for the time.

this is a natural reaction.

suppose finishing.

aren't you true to it?

where is blue in this mixture of sunlight and darkness

;

why does daytime get two of them

?

give up

I live in a mountain town where

the queers are beaten by rednecks and cops alike

out in the open,

where bums become progressively aggressive,

where heat and tourism rise annually,

where rent reflects upper class assets

when the working class is seeking shelter without snowy beds,

where the more educated work service industry jobs

for the less educated gift-babies,

where revolution is led by the mentally handicapped,

where the anarchists read books pertaining to political correctness

followed by nothing,

where the true anarchists give up,

where food costs too much and it is now illegal for restaurants

to buy from uninspected farmers,

where farms are repossessed,

where pet stores cater to every indulgence a pet owner could

provide

but where no housing is available for those with pets,

where upper management can't afford to go to the doctor

or a dentist for an infected tooth,

where people behind engines

try to run over pedestrians

who can't afford a car,

are unwilling to be in debt for one,

disagree with using fossil fuel to haul their asses around,

and make the responsible decision to walk in the rain

beside roads that have no drainage system

so cars send waves over the walkers,

drenching them in rage,

where every inch of inventiveness

is taken as gimmick,

where good music is invented and no one listens,

where the worst music is perpetuated with honors,

where everyone fucks everyone

and we all wish for death

under the undying electric shame

a trap can offer.

mouse in a stable,

can you see past the hay,

where the rich spill their wine

on their way to the table?

can you believe anything is fragile

beyond stability and beer bottles?

snake snake slither dry

and whittle a kindling out of rye

and unending night.

…unending night

where the only comfort
is being ahead of it all
with life threatened
but a side to line up with
in bed,
a fan heaving humid breeze
across lost underwear
and skill
under a ceiling
paid with rent
together.

mess

A: "back ripped from suction
to the tub floor
in a misshaped circle: noted.
And, look here, sir,
no beer in his throat
so he thought he was coming back up
...out of the water."

I am in bed with 4 books,
orange juice, coffee, wine,
grass, lighter, computer,
pen, paper, favorite only sheets,
and a phone. and I am naked.
and I have a belly
and I'm (it's) ruthless.
because I am still lonely.
I look over at your side of the bed,
the spots of blood stains
shaped like pussies
still riding raw
on the underside
of the sheet,
steeping darkness.
there is a lot of blood from you
and from another victim before.

I'm worried (not

that people would find out,

but) that my back is too soft

on the outside,

skin cohesive.

but I feel new bumps and pressure,

air escaping, and less and less allowed back in.

Well, there's a fire below the bed.

I propped it up with the 4 books

under the corners,

lit the carpet next to the cork-let bottle of wine

with the lighter that I smashed with the computer

as the carpet began melting, sudden flames,

wine drops, just enough to drip slowly an even burn.

The weed I stuffed in my nostrils,

smell is a filter for color of suicidal lens,

but soon the carpet and burning old grapes are added.

I threw my phone in the fire after I dialed;

coffee and juice will be waiting for those that find me in the sheets.

Out of afterthought like an awakening, I rushed

into the bath tub and began the water, sat down,

felt it rise and flex, heating itself.

I thought it a *fair* end,

burning in the bed,

dying in the water.

My head sinks
to billow the steam.
I, a vision of red,
lively spreading my wild
into the water,
watch its willingness
to go and how easy it was,
that blood with no devotion.

Q: "How did it happen
this time?"

ginger

A red lightning (she)
only wants placement,
to be desired enough
to spoon.
So, she collects silver
utensils and hangs them
all over her bedroom
ceiling, each with a memory.
The lightning runs from
sky to sea, ground and below.
No one can grab onto it
because a static shape
leaves no identity to hold.
It litters the atmosphere with
random association and
no mirror holds her reflection.
The dark matter wonders
where its veins are pumping.
Electricity bounces
off walls,
into windows,
and connects spoons
with exploding blood
and bed sheets,
purple in the air,

blue still in pieces,

and I lay into her thigh

at the door of her closet

and breathe singed particles

and fumes of pre-decay.

I feel her slime on my legs

and rub them together.

The weather looks good on her.

She is still just as warm

and unwanted.

Slow down to nothing.

Genesis, Exodus, Leviticus…

Is there anything
  saucer-shaped
behind our retina
or Earth-shaped
behind alien eyes?
Your balls are a
painting.
Hear the sound of
change hitting the floor,
wood bouncing quarters
as she gets out of bed,
standing with all bodily
adhesives loosening,
drying.
Wrapped in a sheet,
knees buckling under
because last night
he was angrily watching
the sunset,
punting fireflies and
observing them
float down
with epic death.
She has instilled in him
the fear of being left

with her stories.

They set up toy trains

and make music with

focused sounds,

visualizing a flow

of great numbers

of sleep partners

passing by quickly

under the shadows

of the moon.

And we think we know

what is real and how to live,

tucked inside,

waiting for a bulge

to excrete, maneuver,

shape.

We are contrast then,

the same:

black and white,

forbidding multiple

attempts of false

accusations by

common whores,

we surmount,

move,

ending somewhere
we never thought
would be possible
and deciding that
we intended to be
there since the
beginning.

Atmosphere

I am in a room full of balls
bouncing off walls and
rebounding off of one another.
They need company
to have something to hit,
and I wait.
Looking down to make sure
I'm not the floor,
not seeing my feet
nor the bottom of a ball,
what could I be
but the room itself,
just watching them all
from a distance
inside?
I never get to rebound off
of anything like myself.
They all just bounce away.
Can I control them?
I'm just a room.

Trauma-Numb

I pick greens from the garden
to feed my rabbit.
She thanks me by eating them
and she will die.
This is how I've loved everyone –
this is how they've loved me.
And when death comes,
so do I.

Eventually,
our common bond
will be sharing
my judgments
as I share those
from which I came,
tragic.

I found a dog
trapped in a basement bathroom
and, enraged,
broke down one of the walls
to find a lantern inside
that must have been left by the builders.

Years later,

I returned and found a cat.

I gave up and moved away from there –

spiders and my body ate each other

while I slept at that place anyway.

Save yourselves.

Scribble

Synesthesia tea,
the sound of lavender,
pounding thighs
jiggle high notes
of blue 5's
on each side.
Purple vein
pumping place
verbal pain-jumping
taste-humping 8's,
toes counted
two brown licks
of thick air,
play dough
and thick urine
on pita
with herbs
count
sponge-caked
babies' butt,
synthetic motion
of in-betweens
dominating the buoys.
I'm sorry about a
lot of things

we

couldn't control.

You would have loved

this little house

with all your orange.

This is a bad drawing

of a beautiful girl.

Red Scare of the Christian Girl

Days of desolation exist so

that tomorrow simply knows

what it means to us.

If it were not,

we would have chosen.

And it would only exist for the

Asian trunk-snapper and the

Computer-droid Automachron and the

prickly red-bear and the

evil man who pleasures your bowels

with warm comfort of gastral penetration and the

children say "thank you."

Automach chisels truth into the space program.

And who knows it has no further existence with such tools?

Yet, she still believes,

ignorantly denying her own

fuzz and delinquent mittens.

This poem is shit.

I hate Christians.

My mother once found my sister with slit wrists

and a partially shaved head, convulsing in the bathroom.

She immediately sent a picture to all her friends

and asked for prayer.

The worst abuse is the kind that is accepted.

Nègatitè

If someone wants you
to go some place
or buy a thing,
they must make you
believe it's not fake.
I can find anyone unattractive,
even everyone.
With some it's harder.
I am inanimate in a minute.
Without emotion I recall
that every memory brings me
to a very bad place. So,
days spend themselves.
I get high and try to put
on my shoe for a real hour
before I realize I just learned
something.
Maybe I should not be here
but opening my eyes
to a room where
the others scurry because
I am finally in their dimension,
conscious and unable to count,
but seeing all
as they make breakfast

with their minds.

The road leads somewhere

unsatisfying,

for it is still the ground.

death matters

The moon borrowed a fake landing,
a desperation that leaves us drowning
in still waters,
waiting for a wave
to carry us further.
But, it only gathers us
to the edge
of itself –
whirlpool of quicksand
beckoning an evolution
to dry land.
The food is better up there,
a view of homeland awaits
at the end, tree-dweller.
Singeing a cigarette in a sun
so bright,
a black cross is all I can see
leaning against a white house
upside down,
pigeons landing and falling over –
instant death,
a burial in light.
There the blood
seeps into concrete
and stains with force

gathered behind it,

light-years in the making.

I look at the leaves fallen below,

too dry and burning the tree

by its roots.

Catching fire and allowing it to stay,

I wonder how I got here

and feel the need for endless water.

The moon looked into its lover's eyes

and said "I'll give you

every disease

you've ever wanted."

altitude-azimuth

The problem is how you treat yourself.

Death is a slow breeze on a warm

summer day, sweetened crust

under a shaded porch with coffee

and welcoming wooden thank-you-nests

forgetting not the stream, churning up

old soil and salamander bones,

sweet roses cast fresh upon tombstones

and puppy remains.

Gulch munching clam pimples,

fungal tides cum soil for washing

the night below.

A fetish returns to mollusk,

carpet, the unclean.

If a way to view is learned,

dark matter may lead us

to a better understanding,

a tangible way of existing proper

in the function of our Universe,

extending our presence

once we have aligned with the center

of our Galaxy.

Gas

    stations next to highway.

Hope

    they have trashcans.

Rock

    back and forth,
blood pumping oxygen to brain,

and work up.

Coating darts in Spanish Fly

secreted straight from suave

young skin, hot over sun-sand,

thrust them into strangers and weight.

We were conditioned to see

these light frequencies species ago.

How can we view other matter, o' calculations?

My greatest, repeated fear

when youngest

was held in the dark,

and the sound of my parent's

stepped feet were safety.

These are after-dinner

breakfast plans

in a 24 hour lifespan.

soil flies

the
cosmic wrapper
cluster forage
of unending
delinquency
regards us,
victims.
equality is a field
worth waiting for,
planetary flower petals
run through fingers
in unborn dimensions,
awakening the retrograde,
pollinating the sky.
Earth is
a planet with neighbors,
part of a collective galaxy
and universe.
It must feed
its distant relatives
atoms and elements
one day
when it explodes.
this is where the dead go.
soil flies.

summer begins

A cool night of belly-breeze,
shamanistic-tentacle suctions
and helmets filled with
absinthe oranges
grimace curly soft spots
on back of head,
innocence before the poison.

cumming bullets

I went to a séance of sound
and a hippie with a gold crown
asked me to go the basement,
   a Masonic fallout shelter
   lingering world wars
   in Temple,
She told me to fuck her on the ping-pong table.
Mind and shower said no
But I've played in mud before and
I had a condom anyway.
Everyone, when still and in subtle light,
shows what they are fighting with,
keeps me in the shadows.
Everything is looking for a friction
that fits.

Mr. 27's

night quest,
a vision of patrimony,
eventual
perplexed sensations
of armpit hair found
in ass cracks
the morning after.
black pepper-scented
car washes
grabbing flesh that isn't there,
that walks like a nomad,
talks like a fish of the sea –
creation.
I remember the beginning
of a last love,
relive horrors and triumphs,
the invention of asbestos
and asbestos removal,
a fix.
rain
follows.
I have choke stains.

ice-filled dildos explore
shadow figures

who

often

enter various realms of

frozen numb splinters

and, like the swimming fish,

never dry.

walk your sheets

through streets

in your dreams

with eyes only squinted,

feverishly away

from the rage,

and cut down

behind the drone church,

carrying your instruments

past outstretched bodies

to the feared

red and green

sweet

prickly

fruit

attached to your eyes.

the scariest part is

wrapping up your normal food

for later.

fish skin

An aquarium made of flesh,

golden fish holding fluids,

containment of swimmers –

caves of veins and fat drip.

Ancestry, socks, and appliances

do your timeless –

(your black

    white

even faint

    green

between the blood.)

Everything

doesn't just change

but gets worse.

So, if you have

something good

ride it out.

If you don't,

just stay a night.

It is butter

to die of

nothing.

Churn.

Christians have swallowed

the flesh of a christ.

Jews drink of the vile,

wine turned before the

Savior's miracle.

It is still the semen

from the whale of Jonah.

Fluids with transposing take.

But, I have a bottle that remains

the same.

It floats the seas with blank scrolls.

the landlord busted his loads at 60 and now his children travel India collecting statues and buying Cadillacs – creating with innate substance

you manifest what you pulsate;

and

if the desires you're attempting to satisfy

(the Aurelius way)

aren't fulfilled, it is not because you do not pulsate

(the Alpha wave).

everyone is composed

of the same vibrating things

arranged differently

by frequency.

black channel,

white channel,

donkey channel,

soap dish.

pig eyes,

flat tummies,

earthquakes,

fishsticks.

drunks fighting

war witches

hungry tomatoes in

glass ditches

under blue skies

of ourselves

and no way to move it.

you manifest what you pulsate;

so the rocks get raked.

you can spend an hour and a half rubbing

the center of your ass sweat on a vinyl seat,

mixing with non-admitted substances

leaking from the depths as you rock.

bust a load all down yourself

with your freed genitals now pillows

from freshly ripped and annihilated flesh

and oncoming cars,

guide the sailboat in to the clanging of ancient bells,

clean up and wipe the ass,

the waves squinting bold return,

go outside and help the landlord clean for fire code

pay rent early

meet a man that comes into your house to replace a battery,

the fresh still scent.

and the landlord pays a twenty,

you nurse your spider bite and return to the chair.

you manifest what you pulsate.

smoke in her hair

Who is anybody?
Don't be scared
sweetness.
It's just
something.

Mystic rides
shining, ass cheeks
turning under
star flare
hitting tonight
over cloudless desert,
suns showing power
of elsewhere,
ours moving to and from
lunar cavity, full,
breeching
and sending dust
weightless into the sky,
swirling less
    (and less)
atmosphere
as a striking viper
from the sand below,
engine heard for

fewer
(and fewer)
miles.

Bug Boy

just shit a rainstorm
and we came at the same time.
almost a month in the works
saw her true strain,
vivid terror in shrills and keep;
there a shadow on death
builds a misery recumbent.

wipe pain from your eyes
and ring the towel dry;
someone is standing over the grave
who will one day be flowers
or Twinkie cream.
crunch the ground,
squish a worm.
what can we do but walk, sit, or die?
the ones who decide what sounds we make
hear the emittance.
capture, identify, recreate
strummed guitar.
was it you who made that sound?
hammered steel with shotgun shells,
have you prehension?
we'll never even know
that we are sound

and have no control.

wones to find an old picture locket

in an antique shoppe

with a depiction of Jesus inside

and on the side opposite his face

"I Didn't Do It"

so that I can believe in the past.

there was so much camel toe back then,

desert creations, myths for power,

species other from Earth and not

but someone had use of all this,

has used all of this

to be in control.

their sounds have been in forms of fascist dialect,

religious warning, feared political decay,

own what is theirs after the fire ashes dim.

stomping sand and virgins into oblivion,

ride to heaven

singeing with another's stolen tongue

and my sole fell apart from the leather

Love is mowing a yard,

hopping on and just riding,

zoned out on a line

on a motor

of destruction,

blades and fury,

red and green

then brown,

pushing manually the rough corners

and hard to reach hills, areas,

trimming the edges with a care

that burns your back.

worth it.

Love is like scrambled eggs:

something that came out of an asshole

can make you breakfast.

When you leave,

love is like a motorcycle:

I don't have one.

death strut

the developed desires
you come to address with your life
will at some point and possibly repeatedly
let you down
and then you won't know what you want
and you'll be open to what finally takes you
out.
scrotum lips wafting fish into the air,
they're from the sea,
we're from the sand.
somehow we are reproduced,
but they are formed.
nylon chemistry set
dangling hemorrhoidal cunnilingus chains
riding handlebars of the pink motorcycle
strapped to the road
and a hole
and a ditch
and a pole;
a noose is born each town you wait.

angel hair

It has been raining
for weeks now.
I buy groceries
and they rot
in the refrigerator.
I stare
at the falling rain
coming
during the night,
day,
when it's cloudy,
and sunny.
The ground is not wet
and something
keeps whispering,
"We're here."

i'M STILL CURIOUS ABOUT mY CITY

Scare-tactic doom
stares static gloom
in ecstatic, spastic
and expansive
gaseous fumes.
Enamel capsule tomb
tender nerves
turning blue under you
where there was a tooth
chewing gravy
at an orange
vintage booth
in a diner that smells
like poop
reminds
that you
dropped your pen
long ago
and now
you are
what everyone
is staring into
instead of
their plate
of food.

A caged bridge
built with glue
kept me coming
to you.
Legs, move!
Unlike the bridge,
you're not built with goo
and a hard twist
in every screw
like the sex
that made you.
Humans, what holds
            you
is that   you
love   you
have to   chew.
I don't know why
I've been rhyming lately.
I guess it is because
my mouth isn't bleeding
as much,
tyrannical spew.
Run off.

Healing Vibrevolutions & Vibrotations

Chicken-flavor behavior the finger.

She'll make you bite your gums,

nibble your cheeks raw like a dwarf-hamster

burrowing nightly a cave of dental delirium,

tonsils affected.

Tiny specks turn protein

like jellyfish.

Teeth sink like America, a ritual

emerging from bombardment of comfort,

rape.

Chew the fat, your own

until there is none left,

then the others.

Letting your eyes cross, follow

your new world.

Envision what is there

as a peculiarity only because

the opposite eye is looking.

The eyes of another are even farther.

Stretch your pain.

Flush a gain.

pop

night in bell blue

brass as the moment the sea bottoms

on a ride down in a bubble from a fluke

tarantula fart in the momentary desert

of a rural Tennessee river

beginning autumnal screaming

"BABY" and childhood state of "TEETH"

bathing guilt in flowers and delivery food

trucking fingers in and out and back in

never let go of all those fingers

they smell like sour cream and onion potato chips

and licorice socks

all those fingers grabbed noses for the first time

and felt infant tummies

but they're in a truck

dry as piss in a tarantula fart

floating to the bottom of the sea

striking a rhythm of

exploding light

I can act comfortably in the solace of the unknown

I dream in the horror of Jeroboam
awakening his monument for the fury
it lets none escape
head of three though I know there are others
each one a leader

am I Solomon
or are you just projecting?
I am being taught about this present war.

we got there by water
unintentionally
now the gates shut
no way out but to chant
JER O BO AM
the keeper of dreams
JER O BO AM
honorary bullshit interpreter stuck
in a wolf on a stone wall

JER O BO AM, can you interpret dreams
as your Father?
"No."
Interpret!
"Your dream is of Death."

then I will slowly die

as water ceases to drop,

a dry river running

on ash and suicide.

smell my blood pie,

lonely as buying potato chips

in a convenience store

3PM on Thanksgiving

in smoke of Gatlin and cigarettes

The Crest: Thought occurs when the body wills,

amazed and unexplained

the maize in the

the cave I've created.

Medictation II

"She looks like she smelled" the psychology.
The musk of past never spoke of cantaloupe.
But, there you have it.

Stand up.
Stand up.
Stand up!
Stand up now! And place your toes at the edge
of a wall while facing it.
Feel your breath
returned alive.
Then close your eyes
and imagine another you
standing directly behind.
Now the back of your head
is the wall.
Pretend, motion, further
that (after) the self behind
breathes another
slightly taller you
and a procession of
gradual hair-breathers
wafting the scent of
your scalp released
rises to the sun,

its flames breathing down.
Now follow the solar flare
through your heads
in the midst of deep space,
past planets, down,
back to you
and keep your selves
going smaller
in forward procession
until
you are soil,
connected.

Breathe all together now.
Sync, below and above.
Let the wavering of inhalation
wander as it will for a moment
as cars, wind-blown trees,
moon-drawn waves of salt water,
bustling variations of inner city,
"Gelato!"
"NO! Ice cream!"
honks and screams.
And take back those variations,
relishing in your world,

fermenting the cosmos

with   something

on a lucky rotation

of blown apart rock.

Don't forget the cows.

Ice cream eaters!

there is an apparent
and poignant need for dichotomy
without ideal vices
in the plethora of
related blood
bubbling with sugar
thick as internet addiction
coming in the faces of
children,
grandmothers,
and the comradery
experienced in denial
of told obliteration,
nothing unique
about a candy shop
except the bombs downstairs.

dick-sized urethra
fuming
loudly
the world within,
a growing society
of amnestic bliss,
like a yeast
but a disease

in your big wooden room

eating cookies

with girls in flower print

sun dresses

and ankles showing

in the wind

secreted through said urethra

stomach nut leaking

through a hole in the bottom of a cone.

you're not real so you can be

by what they appear not to find
the storyline of truth makes itself available:

the bodies they don't find
the casket not pictured
the tomb they cannot find

there is sand blowing through fingers
in the desert war wind
but the problems are
in New York City

the bodies they can not find
the casket not pictured
the tomb they cannot find

if you want people to believe in the sky in 2015
you have to recreate it

or believe:
in a god
so the religions can still control
at least some of the masses
dividing them enough to compromise
a true picture of a god that could create us all
he chose me not you

he spilled blood for me
I spill blood for him
she designed me as a sage
she encompasses my love
my fury and pace

the bodies they can not find
the casket not pictured
the tomb they cannot find

or even remember.

fly

multiverse re-upload together
avenue of lucid dreaming,
keeping it all on track and relatable,
time unaware.

the denim burn she obtained
from woodsmen double penetration
will last the tobacconist education,
eagle of the end times
fucking
fucking
fucking.

you never know the ocean

seated
holding the largest wooden rifle
aimed at the sky
white-haired fingers
on the stock at eye level
fixed in eagle complex
at the nose
with a Pinocchio doll
resting next to the chair
seated

to Eagle
the doll said, "when
I asked if you're jewelry was new
you were offended
but I was concealing truth
that your eyes had something new in them."

midnight me.

I would say it is lonely spending every holiday alone
sometimes with roommates in separate rooms
I get told I should take days off
what for
to sit alone in my separate room
or my separate outside
I could go to my separate country out past the hills
that are mine as I pass them and then separate again
no I don't get birthday presents
or smell a tree
or a kiss at midnight
but I lean to kiss you all separately

I left off with you in a place in my heart
that looks like a bar
so I covered your car
with flowers
and some paper that rain dissolved into mystery
that looks like a place in my heart
that rains like a bar
but the point is
I left off with you

every day I still make myself a nice breakfast
and eat it without you
still with the belief that a girl who likes Lucero

couldn't possibly love a boy who doesn't like Lucero

but that belief is a mystery

that looks like your covered car

and rain at midnight

dissolving my kiss as I lean in to

leave off with you

iris yeh

every day i
Move i
Meditate i
Expound upon the vibrations of the unknown i

unwilling trod
like a thing that belongs to white people
in a leftover beer in a leftover situation like
a thing that belongs
to white
people
inner violence breaks free
when slavery is passed around openly

the owners are but froth,
selling assurance in a product
but always dissolving when you're not looking

snow on a chin of a screaming infant
saw no one achieve mean crying

a plant that welcomes bees
moves in the wind and towards the sky
green ochre oceans and
wind helm rusty lightning riding by
close bees and meditation

expounding on the vibrations

of unknown

pineal radiation

impalpable palmed favors

sealing breath sent seething

through baked hissing gills

lungs the only teeth it will ever have left

devouring and enzymatic self-digestion

what you eat always eats you

image projection from the corpse wax

in a clouded stench of aristocratic behavior

that inner violence can never belong

without the unwilling trod of leftover white people

all the plant can do is break free and seed

the war on secret places

is the heart that spares not
is a finger of unrelenting doom
is paranoia in the hands of all believers
cocking a torrential smatter of oil in water
on a face of planets disregarding inevitable tombs
passing through beginnings in undocumented heaves
through you and your body, your judge and law,
your nauseous bruises.

each society is a river
into which you may step,
if you form belief for things
like societies.
truth is always in a wormhole.

Mr. 32's

remnants of a second body,

some fuck affairs

pin me against an

old wall with memory of you.

I hear you're going to be a therapist

forgetting what a lover remembers

you working out on his body.

last I heard we agreed you'd save your world

by chipping away your own iceberg

to float a direction like away.

I imagined it must be night when you do this

with nods of bravery by onlooking polar bears.

even giants with incestuous wild

are afraid of being stranded,

but you'll melt with the currents

and float upon the salt and ether.

Mr. 27's, we must be Mr. 32's by now.

I just had another younger you

who hasn't developed her magic yet.

I didn't have to floor her by her nipples,

and though we held hands in the sun

I still feel the warmth through your hair in

Montford air in the spring of our torment and delight.

we were full of regenerating and frustration.

I was living in a closet 5 years ago.

there is no address between it all.

I'm running around

every once in a while chirping your name

watching familiar eyes turn to prisms

and we all close them together

to remember drowning by your body

with what you'd do with it

with all that LIGHT

for it

to it

for us (like willingly losing it)

in a sack of everything we've ever owned on a timed floor,

your knees bending the hardwood

like ancient amalgamation of compressed ice.

Drunky Tammy

When the drinks are half price
you wake up half empty
pink paint on all your clothes
a dead squirrel put out of its misery
as it writhed the streets silly
erect eagerness to
live and run back home.
But I landed the rock
that idled the way.
We then tore through the old house
broke the television
with found objects, smash.
It was her last night here
when the drinks are half price.
We've shared a few of each,
parting and farewells coupled
in heartache continuum.
There is a new sign
in our living room
that tells us not to park in there
but gives us the hours that we can
if we obtain a pass.
What the hell happened...
and what a commonality
to lose cigarettes.

We are promised
the world
when we're drunk
and wake up to find
we just don't want it.

stuck in the rain without an umbrella

because sometimes you'll pull a blank
piece of paper from a stack of inked
when you need to write,
you must remember not to let morning worry.

we have a leftover urge
upon awakening of panic
driven by unsurety in hunting
and gathering

and sometimes choosing a wrong
just means we forget
to distinguish the difference.

:

the crowd started yelling
and I heard glass breaking everywhere
in the darkness
like a giant festival on one street corner,
then screams, but of horrific excitement.

they were throwing something
not quite opaque, and
as soon as the Mother's screams
became my attention
what the crowd was tossing around

was quickly forgotten,

plainly a baby mixing

its own blood into broken glass

and a lost mother

raped by the judgment of the world

lingering without thought

in toxified oxygen

looming the grit of rules and games.

:

the house my Father built is up for sale

and he is crashing into a car of an irate man

trying to get away from the psychotic crowd,

but so much a part of it himself, we duck

under the dashboard. someone is called for aid

but it is too late. the house is for sale by those

who bought it when we outgrew

the accomplishment,

and it's my only time to go back

where I never belong,

dripping.

the war on secret places

is the heart that spares not

is a finger of unrelenting doom

is paranoia in the hands of all believers

cocking a torrential smatter of oil in water

on a face of planets disregarding inevitable tombs

passing through beginnings in undocumented heaves

through you and your body, your judge and law,

your nauseous bruises.

each society is a river

into which you may step,

if you form belief for things

like societies.

truth is always in a wormhole.

while

THUD
it

donate

me

our presbyters

tanks

peeled

after Catalan

feel the tundra

than

excuse him

does clear

race right

purebred height

reaching for eyes that hope

you're not lost in some dream

in some womb

but really here while the music's heavy

and all the fog in the world is rising

in a landscape of fully withdrawn images

and symbols of every truth gathering excrement

in the tombs of mummy grammar,

a salute to thoughts long gone

still living

and in pursuit.

eyebrows and dirtbikes

in a globule of humans comforted
by the action of being scanned
you singe my teeth with your scathing
embroidery of intrinsic lust as a presence
of all soft wonders and blistering perplexities
hungering after self until it's a van on a road
near a dustbowl on a binge of disaster
awaiting your sweat like a drink to quench
the dying dried sea in a globule of humans comforted by
you.
I feel wind
but I'm not sure I'm tall enough to see
over the cactus
to you undressing.

with hands:

I am going to seedy gyms in my mind to deadlift my ego.
I'm funny when (I'm high but probably funnier when) you're high.
A staple of the stable point in constant massacre is alive light.
The world is the playground of an Antarctic collective museum.
We have made coffins and cylinders to preserve our bodies into
continuous adaptations in the opinions of limits, but proof of hope
and resilience.

Music is played in the hanging of a painting
appearing as face of a new world from which
you may never look away
lest take with you an added face.

with teeth:

I still remember the hands the day I married
that I may be stolen from the facing music
in coffins and cylinders as staples of massacre
seeding a funnier mind with adaptations of appearing faces.

Life, Love, and Sweaty Eyeballs

Life – at least there's wind when it blows.

Love – where is there my
someone magic
my entrance of blur
starting it all around again
with trials and hushed liars

origami sandals
when you're wearing
noodles and stench clay

one of the reasons
I came to do what I do
is to make what you do
into something
worth it

Sweaty Eyeballs

Just before the fire begins
I saw your ass move in the mirror
while I fingered your tall frame
against mine and pulled
onward blue then green then blue
then black
like a wizard would to witch

you bent to show me those sweaty colors

to push into an unknown

behind a hum of diversions

left to rot by our feet

your sweat salting my lips from

spring to autumn

and never leaving

though the fear remains

a horror of existential love

and muddy ankles

in cosmic flutter of chaos imaginable

through fingers and asses in mirrors

against the colors of autumn

of spring and never leaving

the fire sprang from my body and washed

your stomach and I know you felt it dissolve

something

like fire would

a blushing yeti

my fun is calm seclusion
pissing ocean water until my urethra
turns to Slim Jim.

I watched her ride away, the whole street
until the buildings blocked her figure
from me entirely, indefinitely.
I thought to count the spin of her car tires
to keep ignoring the inside of my
white metal van
with bones hanging in the windows
bones on upside down skeletons
Judas' chariot
a doom beam
wearing all black
red socks
buffalo-hide shoes, slicked back hair
in front of Daggit's Pawn
black barred dark windows
red sharp framing lights around the bars
we blink together in the dark
with no one inside
just stuff and things accumulated
unwanted
though the hope of scavengers

all blinking with factory scent of red light on red sock

trying to get rid of the excess

pretending the need for use passed

and I just feel it all sinking into the moon

the moon I'd forgotten

it's killing us and we're ready.

she went right for it.

Cellini

ever having not,
   I face the aggregation
of strong hope
in years shedding fat
to thin to eat

ever having not,
   strong hope and
will collide.

God wants your town in the sands.
He is strong,
will ruin your mercy.

I contain a disgusting image of mechanism.

slam-stepped into twin fetuses

still hanging from her own

elephantized curse and prized by chords

as makeshift slippers,

she's jerking two men off

on either side,

a princess bunny.

grind the drugs to powder, grind the drugs to powder

pearls arriving on the sarenghetti

a crate of shoehorns sparkling

brilliance in first non-factory light

this train leads to nowhere really

though the sound bleeds domination as direction

sands accommodate as long as water

and waste still fight

a little CO_2 boost on the way

the desert fires more brilliance than eyes

to vision come up with glowing fits of black and white

some titties are magic

and some

are just titties

and when they're just titties

you're frighteningly aware.

they'd stare from every direction

if there were mirrors.

sexuality as proof of innate fear

to procreate without tried decision

the ease at which we come about it is like death

and some tits pose the acknowledgement

of imposed and unheard limitations

like a dick or balls sucked in or a mass growth of humanity

pussing about as a hemorrhoid the earth must die bearing,

oceans of flatulent titties groaning their own tide swells

unaware of a starving scrotum,

frightened away in a daydream

by shoulders with lost fat

feeling a web fall

and a spider bark at a hissing door,

shutting to hide all the incest and drugs inside

a room only the size for sleep.

grinding coffee with a cocaine cutter

because different drugs sometimes require the same tools

spaghetti western French yé-yé presence taking

skirts up the ass in cartoon form

back in the blacks and whites

with Pinocchio noses on sale from the waist down

ginger grapefruit and candy fumbling hurt

yawns into silent crouching children,

a bomb…it's a bomb!

raise the dead for proper burial in life

hang t-shirts and grass to dry together

all speakers crackle

with no sound pushed behind them

planet-wide

new pops in vibrational frequency

séance of death

and an ocean full of petrified titties

ground into a substance to dig up as oil the next time around

fleshed rock cut aside with drills borrowed from building houses.

snooze ark

Golden Bear the Inca followed
It's terrible what happens to the best

goal in the tradition of chemistry map
there is always a quality of life

always a link in division
color and debt transfer agreement

you are always registered like a novel
you have a total of both units

the opportunity eludes
the desire unstricken
an even beauty holding in her hands nihilism
parting drift waves into side streams
dogma dogs still waiting for a precious head
on knee in dreams in spots
as the sun melts us all
a whimper in the frame of Seurat
down lustrous streams
haste halting squawk
giant generations
needing Golden Bear for food
and warmth
smothered in both

dog eyes still waiting
in dreams
dogma in a buried can

head covered in bronze
on a shelf in the mud
past dried bruises

Midwestern, That's All

I meet the Man of Great Expectation
in my dreams, a visit
with a well-read white head
balding with printed literature
by the horses drifted into soil.
remember soil?
lately he says, "nothing
special."

unknown fight

western girl spoke and
shot a bow and arrow
into the meadow
and out popped
a sweet brown grandma
bitch-slapping
a puking reindeer,
visuals image
pizza bubbles
America fattens
and all make it home
to fuck something
(wished) to mean
less or more.
Japanese porn now
only means blurred cock,
silent teenagers crammed
into unlimited spaces
sucking on pixels.
Hebrew chants
run continuously
blurred between
a wall of light
hugging a wall of darkness
with time

as a breath of monolith

ready to explode into universe,

Helel and Shahar.

Your pillowcase is a long way

from their worry

and is staining,

40-year time portal

through the desert,

red cross emerge,

sand and oceans

without plastic,

saw the truth.

"when will their god

blur to everything," asked the turtle.

"when we eat,"

answered the pre-butchered pig.

western girl spoke,

"I don't exist

in the world

right now

for love.

whatever you do

that is great

will be disregarded

by someone

who hates

what you've done.

and
you
have
enemies."

detox

Going to check on my ancient tobacco growth,

I took the pup to take a shit while I flossed on the walk,

I decided to keep flossing past the blood, gray and brown,

and go all through a second time until I tasted the parts

of my mouth confusing itself with digestion.

The dog shit, wiped hay over, and then shit again,

hunching her lower back like a cowboy

riding hard in slim, slow motion;

send it to the dirt.

A second cleanse to relieve the tension,

it is Sunday, spring time; and the puss in the window

can smell the dissipated flecks of built tension

as the sun sprays the deterioration

with our insides now dispersed.

hold the tool tightly

go really fuck yourself,
extending your masturbating ambition
to keep jamming-not-just-rubbing
the extensions wild.

there is the drone of a humming world
fucking itself in ducks quacking and insects
crescendo-strutting into violence
with the sounds of pornography simultaneously
impregnating the desert with unexplainable eggs in
the unexplainable sand.

    a few now come in –
"pure reality only exists in
humiliation"   –
repeated.

I will teach you of substance,
from darkening skin
in a house made of flesh-kill,
speaking nervously on a head
emptied through pictures
of wrinkles in feet, assholes,
pussy, and genitals of all species
starting with the Shetland Pony
down to hare, although he

never saw a camera
or knew of the existence of such.

Everything hangs
dead.

Stretch.
always downward here
always spiral back to the circle.

freak yard, peer the window
to feel the fluff of the street gum pillow
encapsulating the highway negativity
and row yourself down the river you find
to the center that avoids failing to reveal itself
like peeling an avocado with overworked
fingers swollen in anxiety.

Something thinks
it is funny
when you breathe
familiarly.
that is blood.

there is blood
over there,
over there

standing in the heat

with a coat on top of origins

in and of sweat

a world of glands flipping through a single pocket

of cold

from outside,

still, within

the pages.

blessed

Sitting in the laundromat,

brown paint and ethnic intention,

the scent of bathroom rug surrounding

feces and cum drains,

I see across the street

to the back of a house

a covered patio

with a fat old Diabetes

trimming and fondling her greenery

like she'd ruff a baby

into a new diaper pampered tough

given a life of option.

Her new dark-skinned neighbor

walks out

next door

carrying a plate with

a heap of aluminum foil,

licks his fingers on the way back from the car

and, spotting the pulsating cunt, waves,

leaving his goods for morning

behind to congregate the seat cushions

smelling of after-church.

She appears to ignore him like television,

glaring the screen to formulate "the nigger

who can afford this once decent

street," now colored red under mutt brows.

Television used to come in black and white,

the latter being the important ingredient to see

beauty from static darkness, the non-discernible contained.

"With the picture we didn't have to smell them."

Radio voice pronounces, "The African

remains dutifully entertaining

in every aspect of capitalism we create,

as a mailman's big grin, stumbling buffoonery

just to keep the pale from feeling mistakable,

yes sir, yes master, may I take your order?

See, they ask for it now."

He enters his home with maddened acceptance,

a usual learning.

Daily, she hates

not to see

through the curtains,

so curious

when he's inside,

her bulbs of camel garlic,

rainbow trout and thighs

directly pressed

against the upstairs bathroom window

across from neighbor's shower,

stained glass.

Amelia Earhart landed in Africa
and never found the ability to walk
out of the pulsating, heated rhythms
of the magical jungle.

who made this

I forget sometimes
that I am a sick man.
it's when the medicine works
my memory eludes
the hours of chaotic panic,
consistent fury like a city realizing the bomb is about to hit
after a hundred thousand cups of cowboy coffee,
hearing it before it happens,
all the eyes out of sockets before necessary,
mine leading the reaction.

forgetting the pain is all life is about.
if we are sick that is all life is about.
I never understood getting better;
it's impossible,
successfully prolonged
nonetheless.
there exists a dichotomy of fear and
improvised escape
and it's the pinstripe for us all.
is the light the lines?
who are you looking for in me?

Walnuts

the nastiest beasts
originate in human minds
with mystical nature
and eventual irreverence.
Projection:
a means to turn women into dragons,
herbs to flying demons,
human error into psychological dominance,
the fear of death into fire.
it is accepted and encouraged,

control -
first step
is losing.

everyone fought for the Jerusalem
they lost.
mutants created with brain-washing
techniques
acclaimed in heart,
the undiscovered soul
venture violently with purpose
to the next war against themselves.

when I think of my Grandmother's home,
the smell of various foods become apparent

as some sort of omnipresence I usually choose to ignore.

there was always some sort of snack in the rooms in front

and behind the kitchen,

sometimes Pringles chips or

chocolate-covered pretzels,

but always nuts.

Mixed Selection always contained Brazil nuts,

which my Great-Grandfather called

"Nigger Toes."

a rumor

situated in low mutterings arose

that he had long ago

offered to take my father

to a Klan meeting.

at a family meal,

everyone sick of each other,

sitting around thinking about how much money

each pocket concealed,

we confronted my Grandmother.

the stories were bitterly ridiculed

as a mistaken piece of information

so we were to keep hush about the old farmer's

views taken out on the nuts

and only remember the times

he held us and picked apples.

from then on,

Grandma set out a bowl of walnuts,

only walnuts.

evolutionary smell addicts

Timing pornography

for love,

moments orgasm

together

on purpose,

a sing-along

in fingers.

Faraway

just jovial

ice cream

kept chilled

next to heated

brut-scent fish

pickled sandwich,

closer

it is manure.

Jump into

the geometric

glory hole,

and wave

the chunks

goodbye,

licking

reality in

pubic boogers

and love slurps.

Suffocating to
masturbate your
inner child,
watch and
learn in phrases
involuntary aging.
We came to the circus
to see the possible
entertainment
of animal abuse
and realized
we are the animals.
Can meal tow?
When is the last time
you really smelled
a child?
They walk chewing,
amnesiatic,
aged to maximum
instinct recalling
safety-tits.
Good-with-kids
complex unbalances
quiet mood
for others.
But, then we get
the Onion Eater:

Red rice
white thighs
high night
clear sight
tight with
undone buttons
over skin-drawn
lines of 'cry!' -
sit with.
Hush
    and
          they
will clone
a mastodon for
     your today,
     tight-cheeks.
So, spread
your sweat
in toes
and need.

wooden plates

cut rags
to hang on walls
to cut holes
for electric outlets
to cut slits
for plugging in
to trim corners
of time
to add life,
puddling.
cylindrical
gurgling motion,
choking bleak
black education
swivel chip dip
seasoned with
crystals
amidst pings
and clanks of
glass gongs
and mindchimes
inspired by rice.
'If this were hollow,
we wouldn't eat anything.'

Selling empty pill capsules

under Albion lanterns,

tea served on candles,

remain-guide promise

'shoot' ooze.

..drip...

the top had enough.

Rest now for bell

is gone

and so is

home,

patterns appearing

up floor-pillows

into pant-legs

and inside

to stay.

The bell is gone

and so is

home.

kicking air

massive lab retard
fastening after halved leotards
snapping sadly more
bodies of the young

the electromagnetism of holographic goat
   (sea eel entropy, man's negligence in how low giraffes can go)
on dried cowskin
   (under eyed coffins)
silkens the polyrhythmic cowboy
   (still kin to folly-ridden, rinsed cob toys)
of Blue Bird, a horse to let out to run.
   (heart is a cage on a steel wool head)

Knuckled dong chow needing the vicious forest,
air swimming mist (translation) from nostril (point of confusion)
plunge rotation (inter-species origins):

   I g/have the person that took my love away.

tame lords, we have the same foot,
especially   sitting in the dark together,
astro-intestinal.

Butt clay,
   your only harmonies are tragedies.

soft and hard/work together

(can?) I feel this skin as a happiness, You

trusting someone deeply

feeling all the way present

while I

all the way present

and We

closely going

in the same

direction

had a peace,

breakthrough.

socks and heartache

laid bare on the cold ground,

a bed between us

scourge ripples

and tumultuous things

in an acid of hunger

and phosphorous

round with ambition,

sultry chicken,

fill me with angst again

and we'll find a way to do this

when the world was making new parts of Dollywood for me

head doctor said there's no pill for what I need today
and I had to pay him double
for not showing up last time
as I hid behind the front door
with drugs and inhibition
strong as frequency

all my money's gone
into a confusing way to heal.
drinking it away
may gain some strength,
lost coast found
will deny its visitors
while it can

there is no destination for this food,
for these arms.
666 numbers into real consequences
hurry fondly
running to the top of a grassy hill,
it's mowed and the spiders are hiding.
go ahead of me in dresses
to the field and spin
like the grass can't until terror

I hand out checks with no money to back them up

I'm an American now

an adult

I have debts

to the unknown

that I avoid

and there are offices

with shitty coffee

people

jobs sought after

successfully hired into

to pinpoint my action into illusive dream state shock

all the money is gone

money money money money money money

asked as a child
given only in need

I only own eggs,

no rides here.

closer words than sanity and despair
I wound

the steps I take with

entrails of domination.

you may not inhibit the world from wrecking you,

but you can still stand up somehow

if you cling the dirt

and keep the faith at distance,

a shield of walking happy through

cities of amusement

hungering for your money

stooping low to pick it up

tennis shoes tap forgotten,

nervously abroad,

unsolicited by excited little boy,

ankles wet and twisting with trains

down shady mountains

in time,

a flow of youth following everything

that calls,

listening to enlightenment

with a nail in his damn shoe.

bales of the third movement, **sugar**

this pattern of passion and faithfulness
both being reciprocal seems inevitable in endless transactional
development.

the way we accumulate money in place of wealth
and how freedom is the opposite

your infatuations are wet with possibility to any generation,
gilt-edged dimensional movement
a sway of twang
setting the whole refrigerator on fire to get away with nibbles
condiment soup mixed of unnoticed amounts

the skin of a musician is rich
can travel the world and feed hunger
for other music
smells of same-olds
in bars and beds with unwashed sheets if lucky
the smells must be there for their rich skin
it is freedom to accumulate roots and branches, **fruit**

when you awaken there may be you in that room
with a bowl of sweet leaves
where you are now
after the dream of all before
one line
two lines

awaken

you are the one and only god

take and eat

showered and seasick

finger dipping into fleshy shoulders

pulling out the crystals

load

wild card in a captain's body
he appreciates, even giggles
at the wind,
but at the end of the day
his duty is to sail through it.

what is there after sex but baggage without love
the need to flee
love is a function of praying for ambulance victims
when you hear the sirens,
obediently feeling guilty it isn't you inside

or you could just go shit

love is a function of species survival
hope it's global hope it's global
you can fuck her and her and maybe him
and leave
if you have enough money
that's what money does
let's you leave
as long as you take the need to get more with you

this is my stamp money
just writing
not editing
not sending in,

this is my stamp money

not me

just writing

a bleak aboriginal hunger for time

baggy

at 30
I started a career,
learned to live alone again,
can identify the best hundred bucks I've spent,
lost thirty pounds,
haven't had sex this year that I'd speak of,
drive a space van,
morning coffee is better than anything,
eat 6 poached eggs at once,
have identified the need to
be honest with what I actually like,
I've smoked my cum clear,
can identify a wettest lover,
know the bastard of love
and what good I refuse to give it,
I yawn bigger
resembling a bear
mimicking my pup,
I blow my nose hard enough
to vibrate perfectly
remedying a nostril itch,
I have maintained my fetish
though added others,
have written around 700
unpublished poems,

blow my nose like a celebrating

elephant,

cough like a sailor trying to

reach sand with phlegm,

have a mechanic I trust and recommend,

have to masturbate less

and it worries me significantly,

still don't understand,

can explain the corrupt falsehood

of biblical translation, intention,

and origin to anyone who believes

that they may know the higher scholar

no longer accepts script as truth

but lesson as purpose.

letthepoisonintothewater

todrownthehostilevisitors

samepoisonaswhatgotthevisitor'sattention

inthefirstplace –

Desert space to ocean.

blowing ash and resin into

strings tuned together,

meteorites across the room –

strum from the lungs

time-worn jeans lighting

short cigarettes.

guzzle

"I'd invite you in, but there's sex strewn everywhere in there…"

our atmosphere eats what

it does not need, dust

from the outside,

flying balls of smaller sinking sand

a religious glitter of remission.

if everything has a moment where nothing explodes

and that moment lasts

into phase, even to a stage,

all specks will be sucked

into non-existence vacuum's magnetic friction

static equilibrium ensue

no back-and-forth-steady,

balance.

when a star dies

it will blow its planets

into the next phase

flowing equilibrium,

ice watering.

she looked good

and acted on it.

mindfuck

I'm
writing
 this
 with
 my
   penis   written
    to   I've   a
                                                            you.
        show   that   whole   inside
                                         book   of

tragedy in all directions

separation-situation
the pain into
something two particles
go through
together

in the hunger of despair
I accumulate the injunction of
woe

versed a carving of alabaster
towers ringing gunshots
and hope for seclusion
but climbed down
and
well
she left

view the side that feels
terrible about all of it
the whole side
as tragedy

particle blue
I wanted to tell someone
and I hope it's okay to tell
particle you

the rain never felt so good
unobtrusive even
like the smell of your sweat

rabbit moss

knee-licker, the perfect height
for the supreme diet

I started by feeling healing
in any identifiable part of
my body,
first the hands.

 slipper fun into the night
finding girls and rum inside
forge tulips odd in stature
above faces in manure and otter teeth

transit youth generator
finding you were there and only smarter
tall before the boys

train in my body
the way I'll feel inside

Medictation

Revolving winds,
I remember,
red clay under a white
red and blue swing set,
the one I used to handcuff my cousin to
and leave for hours.
The hill never could grow grass
and all the puppies would die under the same yard-house.
All but the radishes wouldn't make it in the garden
and the puppy that made it ended up in a trash can.
I was fed cough syrup, given bunk beds,
sustained a pet fish on Pop Tarts there.
I was administered shots and drank banana medicine.
Things that make your body happy rarely taste great
at first.
I don't think that doctor ever raped and killed that other
little girl, right?
My arm was swollen and propped with pillows
on the couch where I crawled through my Father's legs.
Eventually, he made me stop the game.
I shared my sucker with the first sister,
ripped through scrotum flesh with a zipper.
There my finger bled because I made it,
shaved it with a razor blade,
took a last father-son shower.

My chained cousin shit in the bathtub

when we shared it,

joked about feet with crazed eyes.

We smoked cigars together,

too old young.

She remembers dressing me in drag

to anger my Father.

Don't be jealous of the pine needles and chopped wood,

this first home

the beginning of terrors.

I realized them further. Om.

roll me in a blunt and blow me,
their home until they bleed

I am building a home in new places

and missing it when I leave

on short vacation

tripled death fingers elongated

youth inside forgetting to wash

their home

with juice from the deceased

dripping

down table legs

and human legs

into socks and wood grain

from cleaning towels

pus of the children of some lost god slop

hungering like a soul for dinner with black pepper

singing to myself nude on the roof of

feelings of ass chimneys and cancer rain

after a one night stand breakup

yellow shoe delta

dividing cardiac heat

slop me on a short vacation

so I'll miss the ones who've died

when it starts being lost, a search begins everywhere

staring like the honesty of a hospital window,
a child walks up to me, flailed, and reaches into his pocket,
pulling out money in bills intertwined with organs, pus, blood, and
bile.

"he earned it," scowls his mother, disheveled in retrograde.
"Little-Mighty," I call to him, "pick yourself back into plastic
and be sure, SURE, to tell the President that the next time around
'the enlightenment wheel' be sure, SURE, not to call it all "god.""

methodology of rebirth en ice
configuración del sol en el mar,
la arena se vuelve loco.

flying through the black hole
aiming for the opening in space
you are not but misplaced
shadow upon a rock
and there is water nearby language
moving slowly among the fish
quieting the night
with tribulations of granite
and embryo fossils still trying to breathe
flying directly into
SMASHed drone in a pact of buzzes for
who'll be sure to tell the President
of the wounds of strangers.

launch pad

camel toe camo' tent
commanded
ended commandment-
amended commandant.

drone faucet
moan tossed in
crow-nasty excrement
grown fond of never mint
in our own government,
fortune tell her
for tune smell air
four winds gather
fork-rowed tarot.

kite-drunk

Fart in the rhythm

of mistakes made

where all are formed

in a little factory

with a key

shaped from the

crest of all you've

poorly hidden.

face of the world

choose her, a

Daffodil

who doesn't rely

on biceptual

crusted lips

undressing as a source

of equilibrium,

sometimes getting

jerked off

by overalls,

floating away to grow

on a hill over there,

bleeding gums

spilling clover anchorite.

Walk   Your   Sentences/You and I Deserve Our Own Line

As One,

You must brush your air.

Wake up from your nap haze,

pants-sleeper.

You have the best day of anyone

in the world

today, already.

Don't change a thing. Keep it going.

Sing a window

to apomorpha, my distant sky

breathing wide

white widows,

a song.

We are not plesiomorphic,

you and I.

We simply can not be forever.

Evolve with the consequences,

involving your instincts

in all of your vices.

There will always

be an apple.

The next galaxy is a lone hair

still on the shirt of an old friend.

Where did she take you?

Will you be gone long?

Keep the shit downwind.
Walk
Your
Senses.

Severed

I need liquids
to stop shitting
my hangover.
IT
says I'm glad
that I didn't sleep
with any of you
last night.
if I smell milk
I will puke.
if I see a tiger
pop out
from anywhere
I will shit myself.
if someone punched me
in the face
I wouldn't have felt it
yesterday.
I do today regardless.

I awoke with dark screams,
a fast night behind.
there is a fan
in my room with the blades stuck,
retrograde amnestic green light over everything,

knife

on the dresser,

and in the bathroom

a sink full of bloody fingers.

Forgotten Crayons

I have a current fear
that a car of my past
will drive up with an
old family vacation
inside.
I'm moving on,
defense rest.
Opening doors
with knuckles,
future smell of
socks
isn't
enough
motivation.
In ten years
will I be looking
for you?
Will I remember the
stains and monuments
withered with use,
stressed out of lines
trying to think it is
all okay even though
the rules are gone
and the goal is unclear

but the praise is there

like a teacher replacing

pencil with pen for a child

so they learn not to erase

their mistakes,

which is what they

learn to love about themselves

and what they create

eventually seeing the entire world

in inkblots anyway,

observation as the integrity of creation.

structure

is never a natural state, as

brains

use.

survivor intake

mumbling about slippers,
I have the blunt-shakes
drawing over fish on the walls
in my mind,
rolling like sushi,
the words begin to swim again
with salty life
and sticky sides.
most people don't talk about
what they're good at moist.

destroy raze harmonies
in ideas of rapture
on a music stand rusting with
an empty bottle of gin
and a couple of full ancient root beers
in the desert of Amalthea
becoming at once the goat suckling
and the milk-giver
floating above the abscess of earthen deliverance
as fire cannot be found without
a predecessor

The Witch's Skin

Stark as a raven,

flash-white sea, albino dressing

of blanket mountains, sky,

all white, faint green possible

in strings in a bowl

of distant custard,

coconuts worn to thick liquid,

a dragonfruit,

bright red, floats

still, bleeding

as sparsely seeping paprika:

heels,

all flapping like birds' wings

when it becomes organs

in a drop of see-through honey

from the fingertip of a child

with innocent eyebrows

awaiting a safe wildfire in the snow…

bring the witch.

big banger

round the curse;

square it is ineffective.

they will see out

through holes in logic

only justified in edges and endings

black dress sorcerers

we are municipal

not integral,

outliers to the best

unknown to most

we are the Hosts in this occasion

in all occasions of

human comprehensional awareness.

you catch the things that are falling

from the sky.

Calgary opened a mushroom cloud

from a rhythm in vaulted ground

answers are proportion

under punishment is control

only capitalism stands in the way

when the long hair of opposition

senses you're standing in the ocean

and I am on the distant sky-reaching mountain

breath sending atmosphere down.

nihilism sets us free

in simultaneous mantras and

blinks of sporadic and syncing tabla.

one in the middle and four surround,

one in the middle and four surround

in black dress

the planets the sky energy the sand and the sea

and you on a little mud buying things not

to sink

in a chronic perception of being in the middle,

round

and breathing

in a mushroom cloud of rhythm.

taking and drinking drugs

driving fast

not using a condom but pulling out

cocaine in the morning

eating things not fully cooked

the most developed sense of consciousness

resembles the ability to thrive

and a drive to participate in moments of

danger

to be free like a bird to jump hills in a '95 Taurus

turning the wheel frantically to test this present

theory on death and landing in a car going 110MPH

in back country Tennessee hills

snorting incense and smoking Bible ink

eating cow shit under power lines

a pound of sausage for breakfast

and feast of Velveeta at night

danger the birds don't have

but so consciously developed for

danger

they fly

everything we drank (was lace)

we were treated like fat men

overusing napkins

to ascend respected reciprocity

while the world slept

on our faces

ass-first.

we were manicured into the oval shape of debauchery,

shucking bottles across the street to crash on the curb

in drunken achievement

bottles used like we felt used

full of duty

full of gravestones and tattered pieces where

piercings of tidal shimmers broke worked skin

'til we bled white to the ocean

without ever being able to afford to get there

on our way out,

ass-first deserted,

our legacy of tombstones we never wanted side by side

"Never been better" and "Just notice the difference,"

the dogs still living,

panting on an open hill.

wishing death in a pit of language

poetry for the high browed low life
I look 420-friendly but level with ferocity
my humble American opinion
blinking ink down my arms to pool

floating corolla melancholia riding petaled streams
as dreams hazed into misted seed
in absence of name and security
riding to death on a motorcycle of victory
more a moat than anchor-worthy
the color of charcoal
where there is a place on a seat where lone he lost loneliness
like plumbing and satire blazing in gasoline
rich with the meaty smell of mushrooms and shit

some days are only for getting drunk
evening your chase
a long road in one direction always
and for the typer there is flight
through women followed by thousands of miles between
suddenly on a grey day in a fleshy light brown wandering Bronco
you wander after
and, drink-driving, comfort the
pain as a reference
and pain abhorrent to the system of

what has failed the

subterranean substance,

backing the grain of humility for

gills and acid for

water, dying fish in

ether, an Easter egg bath of vinegar

and the ankles that lead to the smell

without ever walking in my direction,

just a skirt to sell secondhand, the desert.

for mumbling and death

we will outlast race

without a democracy spread in a Crusade of modified bombs,

using words

blinking down my arms to pool

in meaty melancholia of wandering grain

"nothing exists until it is…"

blinking computer grass - what does it mean for the pasture animal?
where in the bottom of the ocean does an end show itself as a
reflecting sun
so feelings being attached with blocking or grasping do not allow
observance
and, letting go, opposites having the same outcomes.

gun fire melting onto paper below showing through the eyes of
sanded desert hills
watching the demographics of Bisbee, Arizona, cigar in cheek,
listening to tires clunk a
rhythm of documentarian lust after alien reincarnation,
a flower next to smaller petals
smattered under the skull.

Chromium Armageddon
a disappearing sea
worn beach in blight, bloody light, a can with time to get sun-
bleached
a purveyor of smaller by meeker climates controlled in a vacuum of
khaki
and carpet stuck to mothballs
the custard apple growing near the old people rowing in shuffles

slippers slowing steadily toward the cedar box

to bleed again the rain on sand before next flight

a dew emerging sancti motum to the cold stone of a dying cross,

graveyard of lightning holding a charge for the others.

voulior

I surround too many books to be lonely
the energy is capable and impossible
the ways of a ruthless night
without certain and most foods
the hushed privacy of death
wrists and ankles as praise for the wrinkled woman
there are veins in 3D glasses compromising illiterate gains
stars in chipmunk eyes
that fast

wishing the game on no one

no single mother with a dream for which she has nothing to trade
but ability to thrive
turn out the light, she'll have a candle

no sand unwilling to become mud for a chance to take boots on a
ride through bog for copulation in progress, smells eroding the moss

nor a son without anyone, wandering among last names for a brand
belt buckle cutting gut in horrific rabbit deaths and bloody anxiety
forgetting to breathe and the chance long gone, at some point
a lost body
glowing in orange then stone,
that fast

never wanting peace as an open street

still smelling your forgotten socks for days after you've left

and it all emits journey

scented old books and sweaty fingers, cracks in them both,

veins in a game trading candles to become mud without anyone,

that fast

speck nail ruining effort

 I thought I was on fire
but it was smoke from my left palm over there
there was only debris
the litter was my hand
I was guilty of living now that death seemed prominent
grieving infestation bewildered in the sun
pee running over my kneecaps
hearing sex noises on a distant field television
heaved through weeds hoped to be wheat ruined with the beatings
of a thousand children, believers

the shell of the beetle is imposed belief

trombone enters from under a jeep tornado
swirling metal and agony among the cows
dimming lights slowly it blows holes in development

I am the interview from a future
but I've been living so hard in the present, epic riff
entertainment before singing ruins it
there is a new job and I've seen my body asked
in a room with a reverse mirror on the wrong side
I am too afraid to look out
white-lit floors looking thirsty
if there was a soul it'd be flopping around on the floor trying
to breathe without water

there is no vitamin for this

could there be a new job
when work has been replaced with the leisure of death

lie there with pissed kneecaps and a clover-hand field of the present
tromboning children, believers

though I thought I was on fire
thought I had a shell

body wanted twin

the reaction to stories about my life happenings are always either
disbelief or depression, always embarrassing for both
so I write everything down in code and let you read it when I'm not
with you any longer
and with that distance you can let my pain inside

I'll attach needles to daggers and play with your eyes, in them
and around them
and keep the insides in the stuffing of my teddy bears
the golden one in the corner always grinning at my stories
and with that distance you can let my pain inside

half wit and salad

organic matter evolves the self-guidance of doctors
the family band of two showing what they've come up with in their
home
thankful for the dog collar though led over cliffs
like capitalism

violet fears in white laced world poking hills maneuvering death
toilet town where pumps run dry out of shit to rummage in a dusting
of dehydrated diarrhea and useless plankton all ashore in the rush of
nature
like greed with a torn sole

like a bright superhero blinding in flight
free the people and the people will need to be freed
unbored Jerusalem and Hades in Mexican sand free of people
with the need to be freed
I make all the world's music and the rests rearrange
hung balls topped off to the brim with floating measures
pumping lost-fun-of-children-fed vegetables
with chlorophyll laughter
and water-bleeding climaxes en vitriol on young hands
and black pepper hearts trading pain for hidden disasters
Calgary in a can, a mountain to climb and tremble

there's always a word of story along the way

hate-knitting euphemisms in a plague of crotch-dried eyes

there is a lake for this but I always feel the happiness drowning

fingering around aged wood in darkness for a way

for the day to remain notched

I've always felt it all

sickened by the smells of camp

better in the woods where I'd die hiding in a secluded

forest pump organ room

holding in shit trying to smell the chalk of distant carpet in silence

puckering to an azimuth already an engine

empty but working like a little atom room pumping tunes

comfort in a closet among ruins cowering the saw and tether

weaving humans to entrails of multiple songs at once

in a chant of dismembered melody

we, veiled silent as coming rain smells of cheesed afternoons

sedated genitals in mantra of whim sniffing sweaty

cash as a room slowly pressing keys

It begins: He was already tired.

when we were young my Father owned several businesses and gradually lost them all. Then, he got a high-hour fast food job at a fry restaurant inside a massive cheap-labor grocery and supply store. My first memory of this particular miserable reality is a newspaper with a villain portrait followed by a whirl of telephone calls. He had shot a woman, a bleach-blonde woman presumed to be a customer at the restaurant in the store. He had come to full capacity of what he could take from his place in capitalism. At some point we all get there. My Godmother worked in the Sherriff's office and got him a deputy Sherriff's identification card, small and plastic like a driver's license you get when you're sixteen and full of reckless hope, but with his card he could carry a gun almost anywhere, first bullet missing in the chamber for mistakes. The day he shot and killed that blonde woman he also went missing. He worked a shit job with matching pay, so running away seemed impossible. That critical thinking was part of my first memory, that doubt of ability and all details involved, and wondering what my mother would do, how she would find him to reconnect, if she would, if we would ever see him again. He didn't seem so far away, though I hadn't seen white in his eyes in about a year. He was tired in the beginning.

I went to check my Father's gun case. He always kept his 9mm in a flat steel case, loaded and facing right in the foam. He was right handed. I was born left-handed but my mother made me switch. The case was full of store-bought danger and strength. I was encouraged to revere it and stay away. I did think about the direction of the gun. When I checked the case the gun was there. He always carried a .357 Magnum with him, so that is what he must've used I deduced. The case smelled like fire though. I couldn't check the bullets. Using a .357 meant the lady never had a chance, such a fun gun to use.

I had to drive my baby sisters to the airport in the rain. I don't remember why, but that is my second memory, around age 8. I couldn't figure out the windshield wipers so, when we came upon a neighbor's parked car at the edge of their country house, I pulled over near the highway, walked back, and we took that car and left our van. I left my Father's old van there and never saw it again.

My third memory happened right after my birthday, a few months after my Father fled the gunshot. He was calling and I was eavesdropping. My sisters and I kept the apartment and two roommates moved in. The only time I remember my Mother being there was for this phone call. He was in Raleigh, NC. He needed money.

There was a bus station in town and that is how he fled on the cheap. I was figuring out his moves. They were uncalculated but worked, basically just like him. I was learning. I would sit and wonder about his job at the store restaurant, how horrible it must've been to make a sweet man of fatherly ethic shoot and run, what the blonde lady must've done to deserve it, or if she didn't, but he was simply at the end of his patience and she was in line of sight. There was a need to carry a pistol working fast food for what reason? Pride, status of a secure symbol

I realized when I overheard my Father's voice that I would never see him again. There were spaces where sounds used to be. My Mother would probably get halfway to him and fail, he could run or stay put, but never get caught. I stopped paying attention. I had held the .357 in my mouth a few months before it all. I wanted to feel the way out for myself as I had seen it work for others. The steel was cold on my lips, the gun heavy. I knew there was a bullet missing so I held my finger on the trigger, woke up that way.